MONDAY

MORNING

SALES TIPS

To Help You Se[...]
Every Week of [...]

MAURA SCHREIER-FLEMING

MONDAY
MORNING
SALES TIPS

To Help You Sell More
Every Week of the Year

Inquiries regarding permission for use of the material contained in this book should be addressed to:
CornerStone Leadership Institute
P.O. Box 764087
Dallas, TX 75376
888.789.LEAD

Printed in the United States of America
ISBN: 978-0-9819242-1-2

Credits

Copy editor — Kathleen Green, Positively Proofed, Plano, TX
info@PositivelyProofed.com

Design, art direction, and production — Melissa Monogue, Back Porch Creative, Plano, TX
info@BackPorchCreative.com

The wisdom of the wise,
and the experience of ages,
may be preserved by quotations.

– Isaac D'Israeli

MONDAY
MORNING
SALES TIPS

To Help You Sell More
Every Week of the Year

MAURA SCHREIER-FLEMING

3 Easy Ways to Order Copies for Your Management Team!

1. Complete the order form on back and fax to 972-274-2884

2. Visit www.CornerStoneLeadership.com

3. Call 1-888-789-LEAD (5323)

Listen Up, Customer Service is a step-by-step guide to improving customer relations while, at the same time, increasing employee satisfaction. **$9.95**

Monday Morning Customer Service takes you on a journey of eight lessons that demonstrate how to take care of customers so they keep coming back. **$14.95**

You Gotta Get In The Game... Playing to Win in Business, Sports and Life provides direction on how to get into and win the game of life and business. **$14.95**

A Culture of Service – Two things ultimately separate successful organizations from all others ... leadership and customer service. *A Culture of Service* shows you how to create an atmosphere where customers will be loyal to your organization. **$14.95**

180 Ways to Walk the Customer Service Talk is packed with proven strategies and tips. This powerful handbook will get everyone "walking the customer service talk." **$9.95**

Goal Setting for Results addresses the fundamentals of setting and achieving your goal of moving yourself and your organization from where you are to where you want (and need) to be! **$9.95**

Visit www.CornerStoneLeadership.com for additional books and resources.

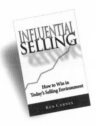

Service Where It Counts...Making a Difference on the Front Line – "Where the rubber meets the road" or "The buck stops here" are phrases that come to mind when you think of front-line employees and customer service. The company's reputation in the marketplace is formed by how that customer is treated by the front-line team member day in and day out. **$12.95**

Influential Selling – How to Win in Today's Selling Environment is designed to stimulate new ways of thinking about your selling efforts and positioning them to align with your client. It will provide your team with new strategies and activities that will help you start winning today ... and it will change your sales perspective forever. **$14.95**

175 Ways to Get More Done in Less Time has 175 really good suggestions that will help you get things done faster ... and usually better. **$9.95**

The Nature of Excellence Daily Inspiration is a compelling collection of quotes about leadership and life, is perfect for office desks, school and home. Offering a daily dose of inspiration, this terrific calendar makes the perfect gift or motivational reward. **$15.95**

One of each of the items shown here are included in the *Accelerate Inspired Sales & Service* Package!

☑ YES! Please send me extra copies of *Monday Morning Sales Tips!*
1-30 copies $12.95   31-100 copies $11.95   101+ copies $10.95

Monday Morning Sales Tips _____ copies X _____ = $ _____

Accelerate Inspired Sales & Service Resources

Accelerate Inspired Sales & Service Package _____ pack(s) X $129.95 = $ _____
(Includes all items shown inside.)

Other Books

_____ _____ copies X _____ = $ _____

_____ _____ copies X _____ = $ _____

_____ _____ copies X _____ = $ _____

_____ _____ copies X _____ = $ _____

_____ _____ copies X _____ = $ _____

Shipping & Handling $ _____

Subtotal $ _____

Sales Tax (8.25%-TX Only) $ _____

Total (U.S. Dollars Only) $ _____

Shipping and Handling Charges

Total $ Amount	Up to $49	$50-$99	$100-$249	$250-$1199	$1200-$2999	$3000+
Charge	$7	$9	$16	$30	$80	$125

Name _____ Job Title _____

Organization _____ Phone _____

Shipping Address _____ Fax _____

Billing Address _____ Email _____
(required when ordering PowerPoint® Presentation)
City _____ State _____ ZIP _____

❑ Please invoice (Orders over $200) Purchase Order Number (if applicable) _____

Charge Your Order: ❑ MasterCard   ❑ Visa   ❑ American Express

Credit Card Number _____ Exp. Date _____

Signature _____

❑ Check Enclosed (Payable to: CornerStone Leadership)

Fax 972.274.2884
Phone 888.789.5323   www.**CornerStoneLeadership**.com   **P.O. Box 764087**
Dallas, TX 75376

 # PREFACE

Selling is the easiest job in the world. Just ask anyone who is not in sales. If you are in sales, you know the ups and downs that you face on a daily basis. And, like most delighted sales professionals, you realize there is no other job in the world for you.

While selling is a challenge, there are ways to make the journey easier and more joyful. This book is filled with ideas to help you accomplish those objectives and make you more successful.

In sales, there are times when you need some inspiration. There are times when you need a reassuring pat on the back. There are times when you need some hope. This book is for those times when you need to reach into yourselves and unleash your sales potential to continue on your selling journey and reach success. Best wishes for your successful selling!

WEEK 1

*The greatest problem in communication
is the illusion that it has been accomplished.*
— George Bernard Shaw

FOR SALESPEOPLE...

Logic alone has never persuaded anyone. If not, why are almost
one-third of Americans obese? (Of course they know logically
that Coca-Cola for breakfast is not healthy.) Yet, many sales
professionals think that the more they present the technical
aspects of their products and services, the more likely the
customer will buy. Forget it. Instead of an emphasis on just the
technical aspects of your product, try to tap into your customer's
emotions. What makes it painful for your customers to do their
jobs? Why would using your products delight your customers?
People think logically and act emotionally. When customers have
good feelings about your product, their emotions motivate them
to buy. Your job is to ask the questions to uncover these emotions.
When you ask, there will be no illusion about your communication
effectiveness. Your customer will buy.

SALES TIP...

Reach your prospects' emotions by talking about their concerns.
They care about solving their problems. What are their concerns?
Find out what their problems are by researching your prospect's
industry before your sales call.

WEEK 2

Do not say a little in many words,
but a great deal in a few.
— Pythagoras

FOR SALESPEOPLE...

As you plan for your selling, think about how you can communicate your selling message in as few words as possible. Why? Because too many salespeople are in love with the sound of their voice and that hurts their selling. They talk too much in "techie" speak thinking that impresses the customer. Or worse, they simply talk about "stuff" (think sports), thinking that builds rapport. The tools of your craft are your words. Your customer judges you by what you say. The more you talk means that the customer is talking less. Who knows more about your customer's concerns, issues and problems? He does. So if you're taking the customer's talking time, you are minimizing the learning you are doing. When your words are filler, you detract from your credibility. So plan to speak less and say more. You'll sell more, too.

SALES TIP...

During your sales call, your goal is to talk 20 percent of the time and your customers to talk 80 percent of the time.

WEEK 3

I do not live to play, but I play in order
that I may live and return with zest to the labors of life.

– Plato

FOR SALESPEOPLE...

When was the last time you woke up refreshed, energized and ready to take on your selling day? I hope it was today. I do hope you're taking the time to relax so you can be recharged for your business. If not, then why aren't you scheduling time to do what you enjoy so you can be relaxed and energized? Start by realizing that something is wrong in your life if you hear yourself saying, "I wish I had time for...." That signals that you are not playing enough. Then get out your schedule and block out time this week to do what you want to do. You can start small. What if you miss reading? Schedule only 15 minutes a day. Starting small will get you into the habit. Plato was right. Salespeople need to play – because sales requires a lot of zest!

SALES TIP...

Do you enjoy yoga, karate, kickboxing or Pilates? Invite a customer to join you at a class.

# WEEK 4

*The ability to focus attention on important things
is a defining characteristic of intelligence.*
— Robert J. Shiller

FOR SALESPEOPLE...

Sell more intelligently by focusing on what's important and
forgetting what's not. If a customer rejects your products, the
customer is not rejecting you. Remember, some customers don't
know there are things they don't know! Move on to the customers
who "get" what you and your products are all about. It's more
important to recover and move on than it is to stay mired in
feelings of anguish and disappointment. I promise you that you
will sell again! You have to look forward and focus on the types
of prospects who need and want your services. That's what is
important. Focusing on the customers who can buy from you is
more important than focusing on the ones who can't. So make
great choices of your focus.

SALES TIP...

If you have a sales mentor, you can turn to this person when your
selling hits rough spots. Your mentor can help you maintain your
sales focus.

1" /›

WEEK 5

Things turn out the best for those
who make the best of the way things turn out.
– John Wooden

FOR SALESPEOPLE...

Selling is like riding a roller coaster. There are the highs of the
great days and there are the lows of the days that disappoint. Even
the best-planned sales calls might turn out differently than you
plan. Why? Because customers buy on their schedules, not yours.
So when the meeting turns out differently than you would like,
it's time to figure out what you're going to do about it. That means
making different plans for the next time. What did you learn from
the disappointing sales call? Why did it happen? How will you
prevent it from happening again? When you make plans to avoid
it from reoccurring, you're making the best of it. You always have
choices. Making the best of it is always the right choice.

SALES TIP...

Before the sales call, plan for several outcomes in addition to what
you want. Develop strategies to address each one of them in the
sales call.

11

WEEK 6

FOR SALESPEOPLE...

Who are your most important customers? They're the people you
live with. You may sell to other people during the day, but at night
(when you are in town!), you get the love and support of those at
home. These internal customers are the most important because they
keep your spirits up, celebrate your successes, heal you when you're
down and bring joy to you in your life. Are you not getting that
support at home? If not, is it because you're not treating these people
as customers? You already know how to do it. You have to earn
your external customers' trust and business. You also have to earn
the respect and support of the people at home. Be a good listener
at home. Spend time with your family. Now's a good time to start
if you haven't already. You'll find that when you treat your internal
customers well your biggest external sale dwarfs in importance to
the satisfaction you get from your internal customers at home.

SALES TIP...

After being away from home on business travel, pay extra attention
to arriving home with a pleasant attitude.

WEEK 7

Diplomacy is the art of letting someone else have your way.
– Daniele Vare, Italian diplomat

FOR SALESPEOPLE...

Sounds a lot like what selling is, right? You can make the sales process a whole lot simpler if your customers want the same thing that you want. To make it happen, you will need to prepare for each sales call. You want to learn what your customers' goals and objectives are. What you can't find out beforehand, you can ask during the sales call. Once you uncover their objectives, then figure a way to show your customer how your products and services will help them achieve their objectives. If avoiding downtime is key, you could say, "What would happen if you avoid addressing the downtime issue?" Your customer will respond with the consequence. Then you follow with, "And if you had a product that would address your downtime concern, would that be important to you?" When they say "yes," your customer will sell himself. When a customer sells himself, the sales process gets much shorter.

SALES TIP...

Before each sales call, Google™ your customer's company. Read the articles and research the Web site. Look for areas where you can improve business results. Then Google™ your prospect's name. You might learn additional information about interests that will be useful while you sell.

 # WEEK 8

Don't worry about the world coming to an end today.
It's already tomorrow in Australia.

— Charles Schulz

FOR SALESPEOPLE...

Selling can be exciting. It can also be stressful. While worrying can be part of your selling, it certainly shouldn't overwhelm your selling. I've seen many sales professionals think that they're planning. Instead, they're worrying about so many things that could go wrong that they immobilize themselves from action. Sure, you can and should address certain things that you can control, but excess worrying does nothing but slow you down. So instead of worrying, look at what you've done to prepare. Are you doing all you can in advance to be ready for what you can anticipate? Then you're done worrying because, once you have done all you can do, worrying is not going to help you get any more prepared. The world isn't coming to an end. Just check the time in Australia.

SALES TIP...

A quick way to relax is to focus on your breathing. Sit or stand straight and slowly breathe in through your nose. Breathe out through your mouth to a count of six. Repeat twice.

WEEK 9

*The pessimist may be right in the long run,
but the optimist has a better time during the trip.*

— Anonymous

FOR SALESPEOPLE...

Your attitude has to be one of your most important selling tools.
Ever notice how you feel when you're with someone who has a
positive attitude? You probably feel energized. Then there's
Debbie Downer. That's the person who knows what will go
wrong, how it will go wrong, and when it will go wrong. That's
the person from whom you catch the downer funk. Stay away
from these people if you want to do well in sales! I'm not so sure
that the pessimist is even right in the long run. If you learn from
your mistakes, how can they really be bad? So if you believe
things are generally going to turn out all right, you will act on
that assumption. Prepare, study, read, practice and learn. When
you do, you can be a sales optimist. Then your sales will turn out
all right and you will have a better time in sales.

SALES TIP...

Recognize which people you should avoid. If you can't avoid
them, limit the time you have with them.

 # WEEK 10

Feed your faith and your doubts will starve to death.

— Roadside church

FOR SALESPEOPLE...

I'm not trying to get religious on you, but believing in your own selling ability is critical to selling. Yes, there will be times when the rejection is hard to deal with. Take a breath. Take the time to think about your ability, why you chose selling, and all your past success. Then you can believe you will do better in the future. Hope is essential to selling, and your belief in yourself is absolutely critical.

SALES TIP...

Make a note of the things that you do well. Put the notes in a file. When you're down, review the file for an ego boost.

WEEK 11

Do the thing we fear, and the death of fear is certain.

– Ralph Waldo Emerson

FOR SALESPEOPLE...

Life is certainly easy when we do the same things over and over again. We get better at the familiar tasks and know with some certainty that success will come. Just think if you never tried something new. Wouldn't life be just a little boring? There's a happy balance between boredom and the stress from trying something unfamiliar. Why not try something that you've been just a little afraid to try? It could be a new presentation, calling on a different type of customer, expanding your business, firing a customer, or asking for a referral. Whatever has challenged you, why not think about facing the challenge and doing one small thing about it? Whatever happens – success or failure – your life will be different and you will be better for it.

SALES TIP...

Create a list of challenges. Each month, tackle one item on your list.

Week 12

There is no reason anyone would want a computer in their home.
– Ken Olsen
Chairman, Digital Equipment Corporation (DEC), 1977

For Salespeople...

Selling requires making many decisions. We all make decisions differently. Some people decide based on facts and others decide based on opinions. There are going to be times in sales when you have to go with your gut. In all cases, if you're making a business decision, when your gut is telling you something – listen. The experts are sometimes wrong.

Sales Tip...

Keep a journal of your gut reactions to see how often you're right. You will build confidence in trusting yourself.

WEEK 13

Give me a stock clerk that has a goal
and I'll show you an individual who will make history.
Give me a salesperson without goals
and I'll show you a stock clerk."

— J.C. Penney

FOR SALESPEOPLE...

As you manage your sales territory, do you set goals for yourself?
How many sales calls do you want to make a day or week? How
many phone calls do you need to make? How many proposals do
you want to write in a month? If you set goals, you have a target
to aim for. Without goals, you'll aimlessly sell and deprive yourself
of the sense of satisfaction when you achieve your goals.

SALES TIP...

Tell your goals to someone you respect. Knowing that someone
else knows what you plan to do will help you stay accountable.

WEEK 14

Great spirits have often encountered violent opposition from weak minds.
— Albert Einstein

Everyone thinks of changing the world,
but no one thinks of changing himself.
— Leo Tolstoy

FOR SALESPEOPLE...

Your thinking may have been just like Einstein's after an especially difficult sales call. You may have forgotten to think like Tolstoy when you prepare for your next sales call. In sales, your results speak for themselves. If something is not working, the only changes you can make are to yourself. Despite your belief that sometimes the customer is wrong (especially when they don't buy from you), you cannot change your customers. You can only change your response to them and your preparation for future sales calls. What are you doing differently to modify your sales strategy for future sales calls? Tolstoy has the right idea for sales.

SALES TIP...

Make joint sales calls with your manager or another respected sales professional. Ask for feedback to see where they think you can improve.

WEEK 15

My mind is like a steel what-cha-ma-call-it.

– Lou Heckler

FOR SALESPEOPLE...

I laughed when I heard this and, unfortunately, there are times when I think it's true for me. Do you find yourself trying diligently to remember thoughts that should be more easily retrieved? Maybe you're overworked (who isn't?!!) and lacking rest. If you're overworked, identify your priorities and learn to say "no" to the things that are not on that list. Maybe it's time for another employee to pick up the slack. When your manager asks for your extra participation, let him know that you are overloaded and you need to lighten the load. Rest is also your responsibility. Think of rest like a nutrient, just like food. You desperately need enough of it. If you get more sleep, you'll find that your mind can be like the steel trap it is.

SALES TIP...

If your manager asks you to do additional work that will overload you, ask which project you should replace to take on the additional assignment.

WEEK 16

To be sure of hitting the target, shoot first, and,
whatever you hit, call it the target.

– Ashleigh Brilliant

FOR SALESPEOPLE...

If only this could work for selling! What usually happens when
you don't plan your sales call? Probably not much – or at least not
what you want to happen. You leave the sales call justifying it as,
"I just wanted to get to know them better." Who are you kidding?
Before each sales call, set a maximum and minimum objective for
the call. What do you want to have happen in the sales call to
make it successful? What specifically will the customer say or do
that will make the call a success? A maximum objective is to get
a contract signed. A minimum objective is to get a referral. If you
plan *before* the sales call, you will know *after* the sales call if your
work moved the sales process forward. Set your targets before the
sales call so you don't have to kid yourself into thinking that what
you hit was the target.

SALES TIP...

Having a minimum and maximum sales objective helps keep you
motivated because you are more likely to achieve your sales call
objective. Making sales calls without sales objectives – both
minimum and maximum – will be less productive for you and
result in a longer sales cycle.

WEEK 17

An optimist sees an opportunity in every calamity;
a pessimist sees a calamity in every opportunity.
– Winston Churchill

FOR SALESPEOPLE...

I pity the pessimistic salesperson. In fact, research shows that pessimists are less successful in sales. It's easy to be a pessimist in sales. I think sales is one of the toughest professions. You get to hear "no" in so many different ways – remember that a "maybe" counts as a "no!" – and to hear it so many times a day. Yet sales is also one of the best professions. Working hard and smart produces results that are usually compensated well. To make selling easier, it helps to have a more optimistic attitude. So use your failures to fuel your persistence. And when a sale turns out differently than you would want, learn from it. Try something different the next time. Even better, you can learn from others' mistakes. It's less painful! If you experience a mistake without learning from it, you're missing an opportunity to move your selling forward. That would be a shame. I hope you're making many mistakes...just not the same ones over and over again.

SALES TIP...

When you talk with other sales professionals, ask them what mistakes they made. Then ask them how they addressed them so you can avoid making those same mistakes.

Week 18

It is good to have money and the things that money can buy,
but it's good, too, to check up once in awhile
to make sure you haven't lost the things money can't buy.

— George Lorimer

For Salespeople...

A friend recently wrote, "I've been working 10 to 14 hours a day, 7 days a week for the last 4 months. Needless to say, I feel like I'm going to drop dead on my feet. However, the good news is after next week I am going to take a week off and sleep. No work, no kids, no husband, no phone and certainly no computer!" My advice to her was to start saying "no" more and redefining the work she is accepting. I didn't think her good news was good, either. How can escaping from her family be good news? If you are selling to the point of exhaustion, you need some skills or strategy improvement. Selling effectively is having the energy to do more selling! Long days are part of working today. But, it's unacceptable to do it for months at a stretch. When you think about how much you're making, figure out how much it's costing you, too. Both are things you can control.

Sales Tip...

If you experience a "runner's high" simply by sitting up, you need to get some rest. Seriously, work no more than six days a week.

WEEK 19

The best time to plant a tree was 20 years ago.
The second best time is now.

– Chinese Proverb

FOR SALESPEOPLE...

So what are you waiting for? You probably set your goals for this year (hopefully) many months ago. Are you on track to make them? If not, what do you need to change to get back on track? Doing the same thing over and over again and expecting different results is Einstein's definition of insanity. Sometimes the work seems overwhelming. When I face projects that appear too big, I say to myself, "Just do something. Just one thing." I find that once I tell myself to do something, no matter how small, the rest seems to flow. It may be slow at first, but it gets me moving. That's just what I needed. Hopefully, that's what you need to get going, too.

SALES TIP...

When you face a big task, write down the smaller components of the task. After you complete one of the components, you can cross it off your list. That will motivate you further.

 **WEEK 20**

The first and great commandment is: Don't let them scare you.
                                                            – Elmer Davis

FOR SALESPEOPLE...

I recently called a prospect for my conference speaking services.
The company sells food products both face-to-face and on the
phone. After trying many times, I hadn't gotten a return phone
call. I reached the gatekeeper. This time, I decided to enlist her
help. I said, "Perhaps you can help me. Can you tell me how you
select the speakers you work with?" She replied in a huff, "Well,
we don't work with the ones that call on the phone." I thought to
myself, "How rude. I wonder if she would want her own sales staff
to get that response." Rather than give up, I've enlisted my network
of contacts to "recommend" me to the company. I will persevere.
Customers can sometimes be like she was. (And, of course, she's
wrong!) Don't let them scare you. If you're like me, their "missing
the point" will make you focus on a better way to make contact.
Best wishes to you on your journey!

SALES TIP...

Ask for help from your network of friends, customers, business
associates and family to help you reach your prospects.

 **WEEK 21**

It is not because things are difficult that we do not dare.
It is because we do not dare that they are difficult.

− Seneca

FOR SALESPEOPLE...

As your selling year progresses, you examine your progress. As you look both backward and forward, you can incorporate what Seneca, the ancient Roman, speaks about. If your work has been very challenging, perhaps in the future you can make the commitment to try new things. Were there some aspects of your work that you were afraid to try this year? Maybe a new presentation? Was it calling on a different type of customer? Selling higher-end products? Whatever it was, why not challenge yourself? Accept that you might fail − and then again, you just might make things easier.

SALES TIP...

You can be more successful at some sales challenges when you first try them on a test audience. Ask a sales colleague to be your test customer and get a critique of your new presentation.

WEEK 22

I try to take one day at a time,
but sometimes several days attack me at once.
— Jennifer Yane

FOR SALESPEOPLE...

The statistics are not good about how successful we are at keeping the goals we set for ourselves. (You did set your goals for this year, didn't you?) It's not too late. Take some time to think about what you want, what's important to you and how you're going to get there. Think small steps that build to larger accomplishments. And remember, it probably won't be easy. When several days attack you at once, remember that this too shall pass. My rule of thumb is that if I have more than four truly horrible days a year, then I'm doing the wrong job. It becomes important to examine how to make changes. Life isn't easy and selling certainly isn't one of the easiest jobs in the world. If you love selling and find it rewarding, you know that you can survive those tough days and reach your goals.

SALES TIP...

Remember to reward yourself when you achieve your goals. Your reward can be time off and doesn't have to be an expensive item.

# Week 23

For the things we have to learn before we can do them,
we learn by doing them.

– Aristotle

For Salespeople...

Think about the things you would like to be better at in selling. Is it better persuasion skills? Or maybe better questioning? Perhaps you attended a seminar to learn new skills. Are you using the new skills you learned? You may sometimes forget that the best way to learn something is to do it. It's acceptable if the result is not immediate success. Sometimes it will take a bit of practice or even courage to try something new and different. In sales, you must try new things and you must try to continue to improve your skills. How can you increase your value to your customers if you remain the same? Good luck applying your skills and trying new tasks.

Sales Tip...

Write what you want to do in your calendar on the day you plan to do it. You'll be more likely to implement the task.

WEEK 24

A mediocre idea that generates enthusiasm
will go further than a great idea that inspires no one.

– Mary Kay Ash

FOR SALESPEOPLE...

Selling is the transfer of emotion. Your customers want to see that you enjoy the product you sell and that you're enthusiastic about their purchasing it. I've always said that successful selling starts with selling products that you love. Then you have to show your customers the joy you get from selling. The emotions you have will be unconsciously transmitted as you sell. Just make sure when you're selling that you're generating enthusiasm for your products and your customer using them. Your enthusiasm may just be what gives your customer the confidence to buy.

SALES TIP...

Discussing your satisfied customers' feelings about your product is another way to generate enthusiasm for your products.

# WEEK 25

The best way to predict the future is to create it.

– Peter Drucker

FOR SALESPEOPLE...

Some days the creating part is the toughest. On the days when your selling is more difficult than others, remember that if you decide to do just one thing or take just one step, you'll get yourself out of the doldrums and on your way to creating your future. On those challenging days, you may be tempted to do nothing or even give up. Instead of doing nothing, spend your time defining what you want and why you want it. Then decide to take just one small step toward making that goal a reality. If you want to accomplish something, your willingness to do just one thing at a time, step after step, will get you where you want to be. Your dreams will take time. Give yourself permission to take the time to make them a reality. You can predict your future when you take the steps to create it.

SALES TIP...

Talk to your sales mentor or sales manager about your sales obstacle. Ask for their ideas on how to move forward.

WEEK 26

I never worry about what I will do if I win a battle,
but I always know exactly what I will do if I lose one.

— Napoleon

FOR SALESPEOPLE...

The great ones make selling *look* easy, but they'll never say selling *is* easy. Why? Because they have to do a lot of planning. That anticipation of what could go wrong in a sales call is part of their planning. What could go wrong? What if you think you've identified the perfect customer need and then you find out you're wrong? What then? If you've planned for another question, you're ready and you can move on. What if you have a 30-minute appointment and your customer has to rush off to an unexpected meeting in 15 minutes? If you've planned a shorter presentation, you're ready. Most salespeople prepare for a sales call thinking that everything will be great. Instead, during your next sales call, why not plan for it going well and it going quite differently than you expect? That's what Napoleon would have done.

SALES TIP...

Incorporate planning time into your selling so you're best prepared for each sales call.

# WEEK 27

Judge a man by his questions rather than his answers.

— Voltaire

FOR SALESPEOPLE...

I see it more and more. Sales professionals are reluctant to make sales calls – especially cold calls. Why? They are afraid of looking foolish or failing. The irony is that the same planning that will ensure their success will eliminate the reluctance they're feeling about sales calls. If you're concerned about your call reluctance, here's the planning you can do to ensure your success. Before the sales call, determine what open-ended question (cannot be answered by "yes" or "no" or just a few words) you can ask the customer to start the sales call. Then plan your qualifying questions to make sure you are talking to a decision maker, moving the sales process forward and not wasting your time. A great question is, "Who along with you makes the decision to buy?" The assumption that the person works with others prevents them from being embarrassed that they are not the lone decision maker.

SALES TIP...

Before your sales call, plan the question that will start your business conversation. Start the question with "how" or "why." You'll get more conversation from your customer.

WEEK 28

*Organized crime in America takes in over $40 billion a year
and spends very little on office supplies.*

– Woody Allen

FOR SALESPEOPLE...

So if you're selling pencils, you've just saved yourself a sales call!
One of the biggest reasons I see salespeople failing to reach their
goals is because they don't know their customer. These salespeople
kid themselves into thinking that their customer is everyone. They
think that everyone has an equal probability of buying. Kid
yourself no more! You have an ideal customer who most likely
will need and buy your products. Define the criteria for your ideal
customer. Is it a particular volume, location, industry, business,
stage of growth or age of customer? What conditions need to be
met for a customer to need your products? If a prospect is too far
afield from what you have identified, be honest with yourself and
don't waste your time. Good selling is finding the prospects who
are most likely to use your products and services. It's not coercing
unlikely prospects to buy.

SALES TIP...

Identify your best account. Describe all characteristics of the
account such as the job titles of the people you work with at the
account, company size, growth potential, industry or other criteria.
Now identify other prospects like this account.

WEEK 29

At my lemonade stand I used to give the first glass away free and charge $5 for the second glass. The refill contained the antidote.

– Emo Phillips, comedian

FOR SALESPEOPLE...

While I'm not suggesting that you poison your customers, I am suggesting you think about what happens after your sale. There is more to think about in selling than just making the first sale. It's thinking about how you can get your customer to continue to buy. What are you doing to get your customers to come back and buy more? Are you giving them a reason? Are you clear about the promises you made to your customer so you can keep them? Do your customers know all they need to know about your products and services to realize the value of what you sold them? If you are doing all this, then you will find that customers continue to buy from you. They won't need an antidote, either.

SALES TIP...

A critical time to follow up with a customer is immediately after they buy. When you make sure the transaction went smoothly, you can learn if there are any glitches that require your immediate attention.

WEEK 30

When a man says he approves of something in principle,
it means he hasn't the slightest intention of putting it into practice.
– Otto von Bismarck

FOR SALESPEOPLE...

Bismarck would make a great salesperson. He recognized that what people say is different than what they mean. In sales, salespeople hear what they want to hear. If a customer says he needs more information, you assume he needs it to make the decision. You never think, "He's just avoiding saying 'no.'" A great sales professional asks for clarification. The great sales professional says, "I can certainly get that for you. And what will you need that for?" Another powerful question is, "And why is that?" when a customer tells you that something is important. Learning why a customer is doing something is as important as learning what they are doing. Knowing how a customer thinks will show you what could impact his decision to buy. You have to have that information. Go beyond your customers' words. What they say is often different than what they mean. Bismarck was right.

SALES TIP...

If a customer tells you "maybe," he really means "no" and just doesn't have the heart to tell you so.

WEEK 31

Heavier-than-air machines are impossible.
– Lord Kelvin,
English scientist, 1895

The whole problem with the world is that fools and fanatics
are always so certain of themselves, but wiser people so full of doubts.
– Bertrand Russell

FOR SALESPEOPLE...

What contrasting ideas! In sales, so often we are given advice by others who appear to be knowledgeable and wise. Often they are wrong. Should you stop asking for other people's advice? No. You should be gathering information based on other people's experiences. Just remember that you are the one who needs to take the action that's right for you. When do you know when to take advice and when not to? Listen to yourself. Your gut will tell you when to take the advice and when to pass. Your unconscious mind has more information than the conscious mind. It's on the order of 10-million-pieces-of-information-to-1. That's a lot more information to tap into. So remember to go with your gut when you decide to take advice – or not.

SALES TIP...

Avoid asking just one person's advice. Gather several opinions of those whom you respect. Then let your gut help you decide.

WEEK 32

Keep away from people who try to belittle your ambitions.
Small people always do that, but the really great
make you feel that you, too, can become great.

– Mark Twain

FOR SALESPEOPLE...

Do you have big ambitions for your sales career? I hope you are thinking big. What would you like to do differently in the future? What would you like to accomplish both in sales and in other parts of your life? Surround yourself with people who will help you realize your dreams, both in business and your private life. Hope is a very powerful motivator. With other people believing in you, you will be more likely to actually turn that hope into reality and achieve your goals.

SALES TIP...

Watch out for people who aren't willing to put the effort into their work. They often fail and want company in their misery.

WEEK 33

I am the world's worst salesman, therefore,
I must make it easy for people to buy.
— F.W. Woolworth

FOR SALESPEOPLE...

I often speak at conferences attended by sales managers. One of the points I make is that it is their job to make it easier for their salespeople to sell. Their salespeople are their customers and it makes no sense to make it more difficult for salespeople to accomplish their goals. It also makes no sense to make it harder for your customers to buy. What are you doing to simplify their buying from your company? Do you even know the challenges that customers face working with you and your company? Make it a point to ask your customers what you can do to make it easier for them to work with you. You may be surprised at how easy it is to make it less difficult for your customers to buy.

SALES TIP...

Try to see what your customers see. Use your product. Be present when a delivery is made. Review an invoice. You may uncover areas that are causing needless problems for your customers.

 **WEEK 34**

The best way to get a good idea is to get a lot of ideas.

– Linus Pauling

FOR SALESPEOPLE...

As you develop your selling strategies, it's a good idea to use your creativity. That way you'll get to generate many ideas and pick the best idea. Too often the biggest barrier to creative thinking is your own judgment. You may think of an idea and then immediately say, "That won't work." You are judging your idea, which is not appropriate at the beginning of the creative process. Instead, consider every idea. Hold off on judging until you have exhausted your thinking. When you postpone judging, you'll produce more ideas. In selling, new ideas are the currency of your business. Without creative thinking, you'll find it much harder to solve the sales challenges you face. So avoid judging till you've given every idea a chance. You just may find that it was one unusual idea that led you to one of your best ideas.

SALES TIP...

Most people are more creative in the morning. Why? Their brains have "incubated" or rested over the night allowing their unconscious mind to process and create new ideas.

WEEK 35

*A few simple things done consistently
in strategic places produce big results.*

– Anonymous

FOR SALESPEOPLE...

Why not look at something simple about your selling that you
can begin to do consistently? Then see the results. Perhaps you
can examine the selling materials you use. Maybe you can look at
your networking activities. Or is it how you ask for referrals? Often
salespeople try to make things more complicated than they need
to be. Instead, simplifying your work and focusing on a small
aspect of it to improve might give you the motivation to actually
make a change.

SALES TIP...

One way to simplify is to avoid duplicate work. When you
find yourself creating a document (customer notices, invoices,
instructions) twice, that is the time to create a template so you
don't have to re-create the entire document the next time. Your
word processing software is a great tool for this.

WEEK 36

The meek may inherit the earth, but they don't get in to Harvard.

— Neil, in *Dead Poets Society*

FOR SALESPEOPLE...

Neil was on to something. Being meek won't work for Harvard and it won't work as a sales strategy. What's the alternative? Forget pushy and aggressive. That won't work, either. During the course of your selling, you're probably adding value to your customers' business. You may have reduced a cost, added revenue or saved your customers' money. Remember to ask for referrals when you do. You might also find your customers thanking you and asking if they can help you. Saying thanks and leaving it at that is more meekness. When you are offered help, always take it. How can you do that? Be clear about the prospects you want to meet and ask the customer offering help for introductions into the business you want. It's faster and easier to get referred business. If you want to inherit the earth, be meek. If you want sales, be strategic.

SALES TIP...

The time to ask for a business referral is when a customer gives you a compliment. Always say "thank you" but never say "no problem" when you get a compliment.

WEEK 37

A cookie store is a bad idea. Besides, the market research reports say America likes crispy cookies, not soft and chewy cookies like you make.
– Response to Debbie Fields' idea
of starting Mrs. Fields' Cookies

We don't like their sound, and guitar music is on the way out.
– Decca Recording Co.
rejecting the Beatles, 1962

FOR SALESPEOPLE...

There are times when trusted and smart people are just wrong. Don't you think Decca Recording had some experts in the music business who made that terrible decision? The founder of FedEx, Fred Smith, proposed his idea to a Yale management professor. Fred was told, "In order to earn better than a 'C,' the idea must be feasible." Yale management professors are known to be pretty smart, too. Just because people are more experienced or even smarter than you are, it doesn't make them always right. You will have selling strategies that you think will work with your prospects. You might want to ask a more experienced, successful salesperson for advice on your thinking. Make sure you include your gut reaction into the mix of advice you get. If you want to disagree with the experts, go ahead. Fred Smith, Mrs. Fields and many, many others would agree with me, too.

SALES TIP...

Pay attention to your gut when you ask for advice. It's telling you something and you need to listen to it.

 # WEEK 38

Success seems to be connected with action.
Successful men keep moving.
They make mistakes, but they don't quit.
— Conrad Hilton

FOR SALESPEOPLE...

Sometimes when things are tough, do you feel immobilized and do nothing? If your numbers are not what you want, it's time for action. Just do something. I've found that doing even the smallest task makes a difference; you may find the same. If you pick just one small step and do it, this provides the momentum to do more. Just write one sentence. Just make one call. If you take just one step, it often is enough to propel you forward. In selling, sometimes objectives are big and you want to make huge strides. Sometimes you just can't take those huge steps. So if your action is to make just one more phone call today or one more sales call tomorrow, that's a great plan. By doing something – no matter how small – you'll begin the momentum to get you moving on to reach a successful conclusion.

SALES TIP...

You may be creating your own obstacles. Set goals that are consistent with who you are. If your goals compete with who you are and what you value as an individual, you will be less likely to achieve those goals.

WEEK 39

*The greatest good you can do for another
is not to share your riches, but to reveal theirs.*

– Benjamin Disraeli

FOR SALESPEOPLE...

One of the fastest ways to delay your sale is to always talk about yourself. It's easy to fall into this trap, especially if prospects ask you to tell them about yourself. Who is easier to talk about than oneself? When you go on and on you'll find that customers stop listening. Why not focus on them instead? One way to do this is to sincerely thank a customer. What should you thank customers for? Think of all the things that you appreciate. When was the last time you thanked customers? Hopefully you thanked them for taking the time to meet with you. Have you recently thanked a long-term customer for continuing to do business with you? When you thank your customers, you validate them and make them feel better about themselves. They'll be better listeners and you'll make your selling easier.

SALES TIP...

You can focus on your customer by giving a sincere compliment, which is a proven way to get someone to like you. When customers like you, it will be easier for you to persuade and sell.

WEEK 40

My mechanic told me, 'I couldn't repair your brakes,
so I made your horn louder.'
— Steven Wright, comedian

FOR SALESPEOPLE...

One of the best qualities to have in sales is creativity — coming up
with new ideas for business. In sales, creativity is especially needed
when you are in a sales call and it turns out very different than
you plan. Just as Steven's mechanic had a creative solution, I think
salespeople need creative solutions for a variety of selling situations.
One that comes to mind is when you make a sales call thinking
that the customer will be interested in a particular product. After
questioning, you realize this product isn't a fit for that customer.
A creative alternative would be perfect. Instead of having to think
fast on your feet, why not have a Plan B for every sales call? You
may go into a sales call thinking that you're going to fix the
brakes, and instead have to make the horn louder. Plan for
both before you get to your customer so you'll be ready.

SALES TIP...

Before your sales call, identify three areas where your products or
services could meet a customer's need. If your customer has no
interest in your first idea, at least you have two other chances to
find a match and make a sale.

WEEK 41

Always borrow money from a pessimist;
he doesn't expect to be paid back.

– Unknown

FOR SALESPEOPLE...

That's what I call doing a good job of targeting a prospect. Why? Because it's one thing to try to sell your products to just any customer. It's another thing to sell to a customer where you have the greater chance of meeting that customer's expectations. First, start by making it easy to serve your customers. These are the customers who have an explicit need for your products, or they want your products or services, or you can show them why your products or services will best meet an uncovered need. When you find these better prospects, it's your job to show them what they can expect from working with you and why they would want to buy your products and services. When you meet customer expectations, you'll also find it's far easier to please them, too. You help create a more satisfying and successful business relationship.

SALES TIP...

Don't assume your customers understand why they should buy from you. Ask confirming questions to make sure your customers have the needs you think they have.

WEEK 42

I never lost a game. I just ran out of time.
– Vince Lombardi,
     when asked at the end of his career
     what it felt like to lose a game

FOR SALESPEOPLE...

I just love the optimistic attitude that Lombardi had toward football. Do you ever think you could also sell to everyone, but sometimes you just need more time? While believing you could sell to everyone is a pleasant thought, the reality is you just don't have the time to sell to everyone. If the customer hasn't identified a need, then it's your job to help uncover a need that the customer realizes is important. Remember, customers don't know what customers don't know. They think they're satisfied, but they just don't know what your services could offer them. If your work to uncover a need turns up nothing, then you have one alternative left. Realize you're out of time and it's better for you to move on to the next prospect. Lombardi may have run out of time in some of his games; you don't have time to waste in your selling.

SALES TIP...

Establish criteria for when you should *stop* calling on prospects. When you do, it will be clear to you that it's time to stop selling and move on to other prospects.

WEEK 43

The will to win is important,
but the will to prepare is vital.

– Joe Paterno

FOR SALESPEOPLE...

Salespeople are very similar to athletes. Every great athlete spends hours and hours preparing by training to be in the best shape possible for the big games. Great salespeople consider their sales preparation as important as their sales calls. It pains me when I watch some salespeople think that selling can be treated like a casual activity without suitable preparation. These people show up for sales calls and start planning as they're sitting down in their chair. Their questioning strategy is haphazard and unplanned. Their results are often dismal. Selling is just like a sport. It requires preparation. So plan, set objectives for each call, do your research, get your rest and then go sell. After all, it's the best game in town.

SALES TIP...

Organizing your business is preparation that produces big sales dividends. Regularly cleaning out files is good organization. Organized sales professionals waste less time retrieving needed information and have more time and tools to sell.

WEEK 44

All human wisdom is summed up in two words – wait and hope.
— Alexandre Dumas, writer

FOR SALESPEOPLE...

What Dumas says is especially relevant to salespeople as your selling year winds down. Did you make your sales goals? Congratulations. Was your year not so spectacular? Then you just have to wait until the new year begins so you can make a fresh start and hope that you will do better. You can add some power to your hope. Plan some new strategies to implement in the future. Talk to other successful salespeople to get new ideas to try in your business. Read and improve your skills and strategies. If you take these actions, there really is hope for your selling success while you wait.

SALES TIP...

Reading business books, both about sales and other business topics, is a good activity. Ask what your customers read, too. Your acquired knowledge will turn hope into reality.

WEEK 45

There are two mistakes one can make along the road to truth...
not going all the way, and not starting.

— Buddhist quote

FOR SALESPEOPLE...

What's stopping you from reaching your goals? The beginning is always the toughest part of the process. Are you trying to change too many things at once? That will immobilize you very quickly. Simplify things. Work on changing one thing at a time. If you want to change something in your sales process, pick just one thing now. When you're done, you can start something new. And remember, selling success comes from focusing on the process of selling, not the results from selling. You can control some things and you cannot control others. You can't control the result or how much you make. You can control the process or number of calls you make. What happens as a result is really out of your hands. So pick one thing to focus on. Do it and you'll be off to a good start.

SALES TIP...

Give yourself process goals (number of sales calls made) rather than results goals (selling $X) to make it easier for you to accomplish your sales objectives.

WEEK 46

The early bird may get the worm,
but the second mouse gets the cheese.
– Steven Wright, comedian

FOR SALESPEOPLE...

Some salespeople think selling is all about the numbers. It's a game of speed. They think that the more sales calls they can make, the more sales they'll get. Instead of being in a hurry to sell, why not slow down and do more preparation for selling? I work with salespeople who take the time to prepare their questioning strategy. They research their customer's business before the sales call and gather information that reduces the number of questions they have to ask. The questions they ask are ones they couldn't have researched before the meeting. They don't waste the customer's time. They decide before each sales call what objections might come up during the sales call. That way they are ready with thoughtful responses and they can persuasively respond to their customers. Their preparation pays off. They tend to be more successful than the less-prepared salesperson. So slow down and prepare. It will pay off for you, too. Wouldn't you rather get some cheese instead of a worm anyway?

SALES TIP...

Being prepared for your sales calls will make you less stressed and more relaxed. Customers will be more likely to like you, trust you and buy from you.

WEEK 47

The enemy of competence is surprise.
– Michael Grinder, nonverbal communication expert

FOR SALESPEOPLE...

This is what all sales professionals find out in sales sooner or later. Even the most talented sales professionals who are competent in many areas will find a surprise at some point in a sales call. What's a sales professional to do? Competence in technical aspects, communication skills and business will help reduce problems and surprises. It may sound counterintuitive, but you can also do some planning for the surprises – and you should. Learn how to deliver uncomfortable information without increasing your customer's stress. After all, you'll have to deliver a price increase or other difficult information at some point in your sales process. Learn how to de-escalate the stress when you are faced with an angry customer. There's nothing worse than going into a sales call and being totally unprepared for a customer's reaction. Difficult information produces emotions. If you have a strategy to deal with your customers' responses (instead of being surprised), you just might end up keeping their business. And that shouldn't surprise you.

SALES TIP...

You can reduce the surprise of objections that occur late in the sales process. Ask your customer about their concerns in their business and if the concerns are important to them. When customers agree they have concerns, they will be less likely to object later in the sales call.

WEEK 48

*Talking with successful people is a great way to learn
about what it takes to be successful –
but not to bank on them helping you be successful in the future.*
– Dave Packard, founder, Hewlett-Packard

FOR SALESPEOPLE...

Packard had a great idea. When you talk with successful people, you certainly can get ideas on how to achieve better business results. It's not enough just to have great ideas. You have to do something with them. That's where your own motivation and persistence comes in. That's what sales is all about. The best salespeople act on those great ideas. While it would be nice to think that other people will help you be successful, in sales it really is up to you. So get the great ideas, then make it your objective to do something with the great ideas. Knowing what to do is half of the battle. You're halfway there!

SALES TIP...

Finding a good mentor and working with that person can help you become successful. Look for someone you admire who has the skills that you want to acquire. Take responsibility to manage the relationship by asking questions and acting on the advice you get.

WEEK 49

Advertising is not believable.

– M. Steven Ells,

Chipotle's founder and chief executive

FOR SALESPEOPLE...

Chipotle, the fast-food restaurant chain, spends on advertising in one year what McDonald's spends in 48 hours. Without advertising clout, how did Chipotle get to be so successful? It's word of mouth. And it works. What's that have to do with your selling? You can use word of mouth to sell, and it will make your selling easier. It will also make your claims more believable. After every satisfied customer, ask how your work or product has impacted their business, team or customers. Then listen – and take notes. After you hear the wonderful comments, ask your customer if you could write what you heard and send it back for any editing. Ask your customer to put this letter on their letterhead. You now have a referral letter that's useful for selling. Unlike your advertising, your referral letter – which is on your customer's letterhead – is believable.

SALES TIP...

Your customers and prospects are also talking about you. Always act honorably to keep your good reputation. A good reputation is a powerful selling tool.

WEEK 50

Be kind, for everyone you meet is fighting a hard battle.

– Plato

FOR SALESPEOPLE...

As salespeople, you are often thinking about others. That includes your customers. As you sell, please remember to be kind to yourself. Bask in the glow of your accomplishments. Take some time off as a reward. At the very least, don't beat yourself up for what didn't happen during your selling. You can always do something different next year. Give yourself permission to slow down so you can recharge your batteries and be ready to be challenged and rewarded. If you don't do it, no one will do it for you.

SALES TIP...

Schedule down time and relaxation in your calendar and make sure you take it. A positive attitude is part of what you're selling. With downtime, you get rejuvenated and can maintain your attitude. It's up to you to take care of yourself.

WEEK 51

*I will never understand why they cook on TV. I can't smell it. Can't eat it.
Can't taste it. The end of the show they hold it up to the camera,
'Well, here it is. You can't have any. Thanks for watching. Goodbye.'*
— Jerry Seinfeld

FOR SALESPEOPLE...

Jerry has a point about making your selling easier. Can your
customers experience your product before they buy? If they can,
it will be much easier for them to buy from you because it reduces
their risk of buying. I'm in the speaking business. I notice that
when someone has referred me to the conference or sales meeting
planner, it's a much shorter sales cycle. Why? They know someone
has experienced the product — me. That's why I offer a demo video
of an actual presentation so clients can see just what they're buying.
What if you can't get customers to experience your product? Show
them your testimonial letters. That's just like the cooking on TV.
You might not be able to eat it, but when you see what they cook
(the results), you just might want to cook it yourself and buy
the cookbook.

SALES TIP...

A good way to gather testimonial letters is to ask clients how
your work or product has impacted their company, department
or customers. Take notes when they answer. You can incorporate
their comments in your selling.

WEEK 52

I've had a perfectly wonderful evening. But this wasn't it.

− Groucho Marx

FOR SALESPEOPLE...

That funnyman Groucho always had a way of making such insightful observations and saying them in such a comedic way. In selling, I'm sure you've had many successful sales calls. You've known which "perfectly wonderful" sales calls you've had. How about the ones that weren't? Were you aware of why they were not perfectly wonderful? Perhaps you were calling on the wrong type of customer. Maybe it was the preparation or the questions you asked. Less successful sales calls happen to everyone. It's making sure that the reasons they are less successful happen only once. It's fine to make mistakes. Just make sure you're making different mistakes so that you make more successful calls rather than the less successful ones.

SALES TIP...

Getting a referral to a prospect makes it less likely that the sales call will be unsuccessful. You start out with more credibility from your reference.

BONUS WEEK!

In the long run, we shape our lives, and we shape ourselves.
The process never ends until we die.
And the choices we make are ultimately our own responsibility.
– Eleanor Roosevelt

FOR SALESPEOPLE...

There are so many choices to make in business, one of the most important being taking (or not) the advice that's given to you from "more experienced" professionals. I think it's a great idea to seek the advice of others. I'm most emphatic about trusting your gut and factoring that into your final decision-making. Scientists have found a neurological link from the gut to the brain. Use it and trust it! I've seen too many salespeople who ask advice from more experienced people and then don't trust their gut when it feels wrong to take the advice. Your choices will shape your business, and it's your responsibility to make the best choices for you. Good luck making the right choices for you and your business.

SALES TIP...

A good choice for a sales professional to make is to honor your commitments and earn your customers' trust. Everything you say, from returning phone calls to arriving on time for appointments, is a promise to your customer that you are obligated to keep. You are ultimately selling yourself and your credibility.

ABOUT THE AUTHOR

Maura Schreier-Fleming wrote her first book, *Real-World Selling for Out-of-this-World Results*, when she recognized that salespeople want real-world skills and strategies to apply to their selling. In her conversational, targeted style, she helps salespeople close more business and shorten their sales cycles.

She began her career in sales at Mobil Oil. An engineer by training, she was Mobil's first female lubrication engineer in the U.S. She later moved to Texas, and worked for Chevron. She sold more than $9 million worth of product. Maura has been in sales for more than 20 years.

Maura started her company, Best@Selling (www.BestatSelling.com) in 1997. She wrote her own job description and created a dream job. She writes about selling and speaks at conferences around the world about sales and business. She believes that selling is the best job in the world when it's done right. She also works with sales professionals and managers who want to optimize their selling time using skills and strategies that immediately work in real-world selling situations. Clients include Chevron, the Houston Texans, UPS, JCPenney and other businesses interested in improving selling skills and strategies.

She teaches salespeople how to quickly persuade customers, improve their listening skills and strategically question to sell. She also teaches selling skills and strategies at Southern Methodist University's Continuing Education Program and the Small Business Development Center.

She writes several selling columns, including "Customer Connections" in the *Dallas Business Journal, Austin Business Journal* and *Houston Business Journal.* She also writes the column "Selling Strategies" for the *Insurance Record* magazine and the Women in Business blog for Allbusiness.com.

Maura's articles on business and selling have been published nationally in a variety of publications. She was a featured expert on sales at Microsoft's bCentral™ Web site and has appeared on radio shows across the country to discuss sales and business.

Maura has a B.S. degree from Cornell University and an M.S. degree from Georgia Tech.

Maura's Most-Requested
Keynotes and Seminar Topics

Selling for Profit: How to Hire Successful Salespeople
You can be sure to look for the predictors of success when you interview your next sales candidates.

Secrets of Persuasion (For Leadership and Sales Success)
Learn to "speed read" the people you lead so you can motivate them to succeed – at sales or business.

Managing Your Manager
It's your job to create a productive working relationship with your manager. You will learn how to reduce stress and get the best reviews when you know how to manage your manager.

Power Persuasion
You can get what you want in business when your communication is more persuasive. When you apply these principles at work, you'll get the results you want.

Selling When You're Not in Sales
Great salespeople know how to get results in business. When you apply these principles to your work, you will get better business results – even if you're not in sales.

Contact info:
If you want to have author and keynote speaker Maura Schreier-Fleming present at your meeting, retreat or convention, or to learn about her individual and group programs:

> Voicemail: 972.380.0200
> E-mail: Maura@Bestatselling.com
> For books and articles: www.BestatSelling.com

Accelerate Inspired Sales & Service Resources:

Service Where it Counts...Making a Difference on the Front Line gives you a true understanding of how personally embracing these service ideas can make your organization successful while also changing the way you view your job, which can help you reach your career goals. **$12.95**

Influential Selling – How to Win in Today's Selling Environment is designed to stimulate new ways of thinking about your selling efforts and positioning them to align with your client. It will provide your team with new strategies and activities that will help you start winning today. **$14.95**

Listen Up, Customer Service is a step-by-step guide to improving customer relations while, at the same time, increasing employee satisfaction. **$9.95**

180 Ways to Walk the Customer Service Talk is packed with proven strategies and tips. This powerful handbook will get everyone "walking the customer service talk." **$9.95**

You Gotta Get in the Game ... Playing to Win in Business, Sales and Life provides direction on how to get into and win the game of life and business. **$14.95**

Monday Morning Customer Service takes you on a journey of eight lessons that demonstrate how to take care of customers so they keep coming back. **$14.95**

Goal Setting for Results addresses the fundamentals of setting and achieving your goal of moving yourself and your organization from where you are to where you want (and need) to be! **$9.95**

A Culture of Service shows you how to create an atmosphere where customers will be loyal to your organization. **$14.95**

175 Ways to Get More Done in Less Time has 175 really good suggestions that will help you get things done faster ... usually better. **$9.95**

The Nature of Excellence Daily Inspiration includes an important attribute of excellence and a meaningful quotation. Perfect for office desks, school and home countertops. A great gift or motivational reward. **$15.95**

Visit www.**CornerStoneLeadership**.com for
additional books and resources.

☑ **YES! Please send me extra copies of *Monday Morning Sales Tips*!**
1-30 copies $12.95   31-100 copies $11.95   100+ copies $10.95

Monday Morning Sales Tips   _____ copies X _____   = $ _____

Additional Sales & Service Books

Accelerate Inspired Sales & Service Package   _____ pack(s) X $129.95   = $ _____
    (Includes one copy of each product
    listed on previous page.)

Other Books

_____   _____ copies X _____   = $ _____

_____   _____ copies X _____   = $ _____

_____   _____ copies X _____   = $ _____

_____   _____ copies X _____   = $ _____

_____   _____ copies X _____   = $ _____

Shipping & Handling $ _____

Subtotal $ _____

Sales Tax (8.25%-TX Only) $ _____

Total (U.S. Dollars Only) $ _____

Shipping and Handling Charges

Total $ Amount	Up to $49	$50-$99	$100-$249	$250-$1199	$1200-$2999	$3000+
Charge	$7	$9	$16	$30	$80	$125

Name _____ Job Title _____

Organization _____ Phone _____

Shipping Address _____ Fax _____

Billing Address _____ Email _____
                                            (required when ordering PowerPoint® Presentation)

City _____ State _____ ZIP _____

❏ Please invoice (Orders over $200) Purchase Order Number (if applicable) _____

Charge Your Order: ❏ MasterCard   ❏ Visa   ❏ American Express

Credit Card Number _____ Exp. Date _____

Signature _____

❏ Check Enclosed (Payable to: CornerStone Leadership)

Mail
Phone 888.789.5323   P.O. Box 764087
Fax 972.274.2884   www.**CornerStoneLeadership**.com   Dallas, TX 75376

Thank you for reading *Monday Morning Sales Tips!*
We hope it has assisted you in your quest for
personal and professional growth.

CornerStone Leadership is committed to providing new
and enlightening products to organizations worldwide.
Our mission is to fuel knowledge with practical resources
that will accelerate your team's productivity,
success and job satisfaction!

Best wishes for your continued success.

CornerStone
Leadership Institute
www.CornerStoneLeadership.com

*Start a crusade in your organization –
have the courage to learn, the vision to lead,
and the passion to share.*